TOLLESON PUBLIC LIBRARY
9555 W. VAN BUREN
TOLLESON, AZ 85353
623-936-2746

1. Most items may be checked out for two weeks and renewed for the same period. Additional restrictions may apply to high-demand items.

2. A fine is charged for each day material is not returned according to the above rule. No material will be issued to any person incurring such a fine until it has been paid.

3. All damage to material beyond reasonable wear and all losses shall be paid for.

4. Each borrower is responsible for all items checked out on his/her library card and for all fines accruing on the same.

DEMCO

The Science of Animals

LIVING SCIENCE

Lauri Seidlitz

Gareth Stevens Publishing
MILWAUKEE

For a free color catalog describing Gareth Stevens' list of high-quality books and multimedia programs, call 1-800-542-2595 (USA) or 1-800-461-9120 (Canada). Gareth Stevens Publishing's Fax: (414) 225-0377.

Library of Congress Cataloging-in-Publication Data

Seidlitz, Lauri.
    The science of animals / Lauri Seidlitz.
      p. cm. — (Living science)
    Includes index.
    Summary: Provides information on a variety of animals, discussing life cycles, classification, habitats, protection and camouflage, and endangered species. Includes activities such as making a collage, researching animal-related careers, and designing an animal.
    ISBN 0-8368-2464-4 (lib. bdg.)
    1. Animals — Juvenile literature. [1. Animals] I. Title. II. Series: Living science (Milwaukee, Wis.)
QL49.S34 1999
590—dc21
                                                  99-25571

This edition first published in 1999 by
Gareth Stevens Publishing
1555 North RiverCenter Drive, Suite 201
Milwaukee, WI 53212 USA

Project Co-ordinator: Samantha McCrory
Series Editor: Leslie Strudwick
Copy Editor: Ann Sullivan
Design and Illustration: Warren Clark
Cover Design: Carole Knox
Layout: Lucinda Cage
Gareth Stevens Editor: Patricia Lantier-Sampon

Photograph Credits:
Canine Companions: page 14 bottom; Corel Corporation: cover (center), pages 4, 5 top, 5 bottom, 7 top right, 7 bottom, 8, 9, 10 bottom, 11, 12, 13 left, 13 center left, 13 right, 14 top, 15 bottom, 17 left, 18 bottom left, 18 bottom right, 19 top left, 19 top right, 19 bottom left, 20, 21, 22, 23, 24, 25, 26, 27 top, 27 center left, 27 center right, 28, 29 top, 30, 31; Roger Czerneda: page 10 top, 10 center; Digital Stock Corporation: pages 5 center, 7 top left, 13 center right, 17 right, 19 bottom right; Digital Vision Ltd.: page 29 bottom; John T. Fowler: page 6 bottom left; PhotoDisc: cover (background); Royal Tyrrell Museum/Alberta Community Development: page 27 far right; Tom Stack & Associates: pages 6 top left (John Shaw), 6 top right (John Shaw), 6 bottom right (John Shaw), 18 top (Denise Tackett); J.D. Taylor: page 27 bottom; Visuals Unlimited: pages 7 top center (David Ellis), 15 top (K.B. Sandved), 16 (Will Troyer).

Printed in Canada

1 2 3 4 5 6 7 8 9 03 02 01 00 99

Contents

What Do You Know about Animals?

Most living things on Earth are plants or animals. Both plants and animals need **oxygen**, and both grow and change during their life cycles. The main difference between plants and animals is that animals have to find food to eat. Plants make their own food using sunlight, water, and **carbon dioxide**. Animals must get food from the plants and other animals around them.

Millions of different kinds of animals live on Earth. Scientists divide all animals into two main groups.

Vertebrates include animals such as eagles, fish, frogs, turtles, rattlesnakes, horses, and gorillas.

Vertebrates

One group includes animals that have a backbone. These animals are called vertebrates.

Invertebrates

The second group includes animals that do not have a backbone, called invertebrates.

Invertebrates include animals such as octopuses, crabs, flies, spiders, and worms.

Puzzler

How many animals can you name in a minute? Time yourself with a partner.

Life Cycles

All living things have a life cycle that includes a beginning, growth, **reproduction**, and death. An animal will go through many changes during its life cycle.

A caterpillar begins life by hatching from an egg. When it reaches full size, the caterpillar forms a protective shell called a chrysalis. Inside, the caterpillar changes into a butterfly to complete its life cycle.

Young bald eagles grow very quickly, but they do not get their adult colors until they are four or five years old.

Some animals are born live. Others hatch from eggs. Some, like the great white shark, are hatched from eggs inside the mother's body.

The brown bear stays with its mother for several years until it learns to find food and take care of itself.

Activity

A Collage
Make a **collage** of the life of someone in your family. You could start with a baby picture.

Animal Types

Mammals, reptiles, fish, birds, amphibians, and insects are different types of animals. Do you know what makes each one special?

Types

Mammals	Reptiles	Fish
• drink milk from their mothers • have fur or hair • young are born live	• hatch from eggs • have scaly skin • need the sun to keep their bodies warm	• breathe using gills • live in the water • use tails and fins to swim

Examples

cows, dogs, elephants	crocodiles, lizards, snakes	cod, salmon, tuna

Puzzler

What type of animal is a whale? Clues: It lives its entire life in the ocean and has no hair. It breathes through a blowhole on the top of its head. It gives birth to live young. A young whale drinks milk from its mother.

Answer: A mammal. Whales, dolphins, and seals are mammals that live in the water.

Birds	Amphibians	Insects
• have feathers and wings • lay eggs • most can fly	• live on land and in water • need the sun to keep their bodies warm	• have hard shells on the outside of their bodies • have six legs • some have wings and can fly
geese, parrots, robins	**frogs, salamanders, toads**	**flies, ladybugs, mosquitoes**

Has Your Pet Met a Vet?

A veterinarian is a doctor who takes care of sick animals. Veterinarians are also known as vets. If you want to become a vet, you have to go to a university and study veterinary medicine. Vets treat many different animals. Some vets specialize in one group of animals, such as small animals or farm animals. Would you like to be a veterinarian?

Birds, cats, dogs, iguanas, and rabbits are some of the animals vets treat.

Veterinarians keep farm animals, such as horses and pigs, healthy.

Activity

Do Your Own Research

Have a teacher or parent help you find out more about these animal careers:

- animal health technologist
- animal trainer
- dog groomer
- kennel owner
- wildlife biologist
- wildlife rehabilitator
- wildlife photographer
- zookeeper

Classifying Animals

You do not have to be a scientist to **classify** animals into types. By comparing animals with one another, you can learn to group similar creatures.

Look for:

Movement	Body Parts	Shape & Size	Body Covering
flies, hops, runs, slithers, walks	ears, eyes, fins, head, hooves, legs, neck, paws, tail, teeth, tongue, wings	flat, large, streamlined, tall, tiny	feathers, fur, hair, scales, shell, skin

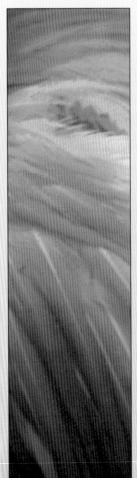

Activity

Design an Animal

Create a new animal. Draw or paint the animal using features from the categories below.

Home	Protection	Food	Color
caves, ground, houses, nests, trees, water	beak, claws, flight, horns, quills, shell, smell, stinger, taste, teeth	eggs, fish, insects, plants, other animals	black, blue, brown, gray, green, white, other colors

Everyday Animals

Many animals live with or near people. Pets live with their owners, and they depend on people to feed and take care of them. You may also see or hear animals in your yard or on the way to school. Animals like squirrels, bees, and worms often live near people, but take care of themselves.

Some animals help people or do work for them. Farm animals, such as chickens and cows, provide food. Sheep provide wool for clothing. Horses and dogs often help farmers do their work. Animals that live on farms depend on their owners for food and shelter.

Some dogs are trained to help people with special needs.

Elephants and horses are strong. They sometimes work for people by pulling or moving heavy objects.

Use Your Five Senses to Explore Animals

Your senses are your best tools for exploring the world around you.

You can **see** a bird's nest in a tree.

You can **hear** a wasp buzzing in the garden.

You can **feel** a fly land on your hand.

You might **smell** a skunk when you are camping.

When you **taste** honey, you think of a bee.

1. Spend one hour outside observing the world around you with all your senses.
2. Write down the name of every animal you sense.
3. Write down how you knew they were there.
4. Draw a picture of yourself and the animals you sensed.
5. Label each of your senses on your drawing.

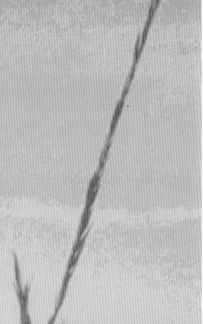

Wild Animals

Wild animals survive best without any contact with humans. They find everything they need in their surroundings. Some wild animals learn how to survive from their mothers and members of their social group. Elephants, wolves, and lions learn this way.

Instinct

Animals know how to survive by **instinct**. This means they are born with knowledge to help them survive. Fish hatch from eggs and immediately live on their own. They do not need their parents to teach them how to survive.

Salmon have a strong instinct to leave the ocean and return to the freshwater streams where they hatched to lay their own eggs. They even risk swimming past bears to get there.

Female moray eels lay eggs in spring.

Puzzler

Why should you avoid feeding wild animals?

Answer: Wild animals get everything they need from their environment. They can rely on humans too much for food and survival. Feeding food such as popcorn and bread to wild animals means they are not eating foods that are healthy for them.

Habitat

Animals live in almost every corner of the world. Even the hottest and coldest places on Earth make good homes for some animals. Different animals have **adapted** to different locations. They have special features that make them well suited to their natural **habitat.**

Tropical Forest Animals

have adapted to a habitat with tall trees high above the ground.

Gibbons have long arms that help them travel high above the forest floor through the tops of trees. They rarely go down to the ground.

Mountain Animals

have adapted to cool temperatures and steep slopes.

Mountain goats have hooves that grip rocky slopes.

Temperate Forest Animals

have adapted to a forest with many plants on the ground.

Ground squirrels have small bodies to help them move easily through undergrowth.

Polar Animals
have adapted to cold temperatures, ice, and snow.

Seals and whales have thick layers of blubber to keep them warm.

Grassland Animals
have adapted to wide-open spaces.

Zebras live in herds for protection. Each animal is alert for danger and warns the others of approaching **predators**.

Desert Animals
have adapted to heat and scarce water.

Camels can survive ten days without water.

Ocean Animals
have adapted to life in the water.

Fish breathe through gills that remove oxygen from water.

Puzzler

Could a polar bear live in a tropical rain forest?

Answer: If a polar bear tried to live in a rain forest, it would have trouble getting enough food. Its white fur would stand out against the green plants, and its prey would easily see it and escape. Hot temperatures and heavy rain would make its thick fur wet, hot, and uncomfortable.

The Musk Ox Needs No Socks

The musk ox is perfectly clothed to live in its cold habitat. The musk ox's coat has two layers. The inner coat is a thick fleece, as soft as the finest wool. This layer, like the down on ducks, provides **insulation**. The outer layer is made of long, coarse guard hairs that provide an outer "curtain" to block the wind. These hairs can be long enough to reach the ground.

Other animals have adapted to cold habitats. Many animals, including deer and mountain goats, grow a thick layer of fur each winter and lose it in the spring when it is no longer needed. This loss of hair is called molting.

Protection and Camouflage

Many animals have some form of natural **camouflage**. One type of camouflage might be an animal's fur or skin, which blends in with the colors and patterns of its surroundings. Camouflage makes the animal difficult to see. This ability to hide helps both the animals that hunt for food and those that are hunted.

The arctic fox's fur changes from white in the winter to brown in the summer. This keeps it camouflaged all year long.

Most birds depend on sharp eyesight and their ability to fly to avoid danger.

Camouflage is not the only way to avoid being hunted. Many animals have ways to protect themselves against danger. Some are equipped to fight. Animals that fight sometimes have sharp teeth, long claws, horns, quills, or great strength. Other animals avoid danger by flying or running away. Animals that flee danger often have excellent eyesight, sense of smell, or hearing to give them advance warning of danger.

Puzzler

I am a mammal. My teeth are sharp and my whiskers are long. I have four legs and a tail. My stripes help me blend in with grass and trees. What am I?

Answer: A tiger.

Web of Life

All the plants and animals in a habitat depend on one another for survival. Everything contributes something to and takes something from its environment. Each animal gives and takes in just the right amounts so the habitat stays in balance.

Chipmunks eat seeds and nuts. They hold food in their front feet and chew it with their sharp front teeth.

Food chains form when one animal eats another animal or a plant. Energy moves from the thing that is eaten to the thing that eats it. A food web forms when many food chains are connected.

A Food Web

rabbit

gray fox

robin

mouse

grasshopper

grass and plants

Puzzler

Foxes do not eat plants. Do you think anything would happen to this gray fox if all the plants in its habitat died?

Answer:
Yes. The rabbit, mouse, bird, and grasshopper would move away if the plants died because they would have no food to eat. The gray fox would also have to move or it would go hungry.

Animal Roles

Animals play many roles in the web of life. Herbivores eat plants that grow from energy the sun provides. Carnivores eat other animals. Omnivores eat both plants and animals. Scavengers find and eat dead and rotting animals. **Decomposers** break down rotting plants and animals to make nutrients for plants.

Animal teeth are a good clue to what animals eat. Carnivores, such as wolves, have sharp, pointed teeth that are good for tearing flesh. Herbivores, such as elephants, have flat teeth that are good for grinding plant fibers. Omnivores, such as the black bear, have both kinds of teeth.

Prey are animals that other animals eat. Many animals are both predators and prey. For example, a burrowing owl hunts and eats mice, but this same owl might be hunted and eaten by a fox.

The lion lives and hunts in a group called a pride.

Puzzler

Do you think *Tyrannosaurus rex* was a predator or prey animal? What characteristics are your evidence?

Answer: T-rex's many sharp teeth are a good clue that it was a powerful predator.

Animals in Danger

Earth's human **population** grows larger each year. To find food and shelter, humans have started to move into regions that used to be home to wild animals. Most wild animals cannot live with people because of various dangers. The survival of many animals is in doubt because they cannot find wild areas for their homes. When an animal cannot find enough habitat, food, or mates to have young, it may become **extinct**. Many countries now have laws to save special areas for animals.

Animals all over the world may soon become extinct. For example, giant pandas, marine iguanas, and wattled cranes may become extinct if humans take away their habitats.

Use Your Senses

Sight, hearing, touch, smell, and taste are senses you use every day, but common sense is just as important. Common sense means using your brain. Use your common sense to match the following labels with the most appropriate animal.

Do not feed

OUCH!

Hold your nose!

A great pet

Very soft

Do not disturb

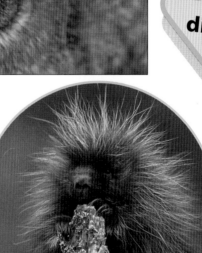

Answer:
Baby birds: Do not feed
Bear: Do not disturb
Skunk: Hold your nose!
Puppy: A great pet
Rabbit: Very soft
Porcupine: Ouch!

Glossary

adapted: having become suited to a certain environment or way of life by changing gradually over a long period of time.

camouflage: a disguise that helps plants, animals, and humans blend in with their natural surroundings.

carbon dioxide: a colorless, odorless gas.

classify: to arrange plants and animals into groups by comparing how they are alike.

collage: a collection and display of different objects or materials.

decomposers: living things, such as bacteria and mushrooms, that digest the remains of dead plants and animals.

extinct: no longer in existence.

habitat: the place where an animal or plant is known to live or grow.

instinct: knowledge or ability that an animal has at birth.

insulation: a layer of material that prevents heat loss.

oxygen: a gas found in water and air.

population: the total number of people, plants, or animals in an area.

predators: animals that eat other animals for food.

reproduction: the way animals produce young.

Index

Web Sites

www.pbs.org/wgbh/nova/leopards

www.torontozoo.com

www.olcommerce.com/terra/areas.html

www.panda.org/kids/wildlife/idxramn.htm

Some web sites stay current longer than others. For further web sites, use your search engines to locate the following topics: *marine life, pets, reptiles, wild animals,* and *zoos.*